ORDINARY MORNINGS OF A COLISEUM

Ordinary Mornings of a Coliseum

Poems by

NORMAN DUBIE

Copper Canyon Press

Cover art: Detail of a Mask from the Fresco Cycle at the Villa of the Mysteries Depicting Initiation into the Cult of Dionysus. © Massimo Listri/CORBIS

Copper Canyon Press is in residence at Fort Worden State Park in Port Townsend, Washington under the auspices of Centrum Foundation. Centrum is a gathering place for artists and creative thinkers from around the world, students of all ages and backgrounds, and audiences seeking extraordinary cultural enrichment.

LIBRARY OF CONGRESS CATALOGING-IN-PUBLICATION DATA

Dubie, Norman, 1945–
Ordinary mornings of a coliseum : poems / by Norman Dubie. – 1st ed.
    p.   cm.
ISBN 1-55659-213-2 (pbk. : alk. paper)
1. Spiritual life – Poetry. I. Title.
PS3554.U255O73 2004
811′.54–DC22

                                                                    2004006040

9 8 7 6 5 4 3 2
FIRST PRINTING

COPPER CANYON PRESS
Post Office Box 271
Port Townsend, Washington 98368

www.coppercanyonpress.org

ACKNOWLEDGMENTS

American Poetry Review: "Wrong Double Sonnet of the Coup d'État:," "At Corfu," "Intolerance," "Hunter in an Arctic Midnight," "Taos," "Boatmen on the River Mons," "Polio Season in the San Joaquin," "The Young Professor from Wyoming...," "For the Original People," "The Mandala Keeper," "Late in the Three Periods of No Thought," "Ancestral," "Blue," "Nightmare with Heat Lightning"

Chimera Review: "The Last Sentence of the Evening"

Field: "Ordinary Mornings of a Coliseum"

The Georgia Review: "The Pasha on the Hill," "Desultory Photo with Ocean Prospect," "Afterword to a Quartet: Vision of a Tibetan Master Walking over Snow"

Hayden's Ferry Review: "Of Art & Memory," "Riddle"

Interim: "The Winter Apocalypse of Doctor Caleb Minus"

Runes: "A Lost Notebook of Srinivasa Ramanujan"

The Southern Review: "Death by Compass," "Dementia," "Elder Gogol's Pond at Plokhino Skete," "Confession" (appearing under another title)

This Art: Poems about Poetry (Copper Canyon Press, 2003): "Ars Poetica: A Stone Soup"

TriQuarterly: "The Pendulum," "The Fish Cipher of Michel de Nostradam"

Special thanks to Coleman Barks and the great miscellany of Rumi translators and scholars for pleasures taken over the past dozen years.

"Of Art & Memory" is for Roderick Morrill and family.

"Hunter in an Arctic Midnight" is dedicated to the poet Robert Thomas.

"The Fish Cipher of Michel de Nostradam" is in memory of Robert Belanger (1955–2003).

NOTE: The Eckhart quartet began with "The Reader of the Sentences" in my collected poems, *The Mercy Seat,* and is concluded with "Ordinary Mornings of a Coliseum," "The Desert Census of Elder Cyril...," and "The Last Sentence of the Evening." There are a few lyrics, here and elsewhere, that can be described as in nervous minor orbit about this larger work, which was begun in the early summer of 2000.

    —N.D.
      Tempe, Arizona

≫ FOR LAURA ≪

Contents

ORDINARY MORNINGS OF A COLISEUM

Confession

for Henry Quintero

The Ambassador's men sit at the door. Her eyes
Are fat with belladonna. She's naked
Except for the small painted turtle
That is drinking a flammable cloud
Of rum and milk from her navel.

The ships out in the harbor
Are loosely allied
Like casks floating in bilge.
The occasional light on a ship
Winks. In the empty room of the manuscript
They are grooming you
For the long entrance into some dark city.

They'll hang the Ambassador.
Then with torches they'll search for his children.
Men and women
Are seen jumping from the burning buildings.
Journalists, in no hurry,
Elect to take the elevators. They walk
Out of the archway, stepping over corpses...
You are listening to a loud bell.

The corpses get up and follow the journalists.
It's unfair that while rehearsing
For death they actually succumbed to it.
Everyone sobs.
Shirts and dresses billowing as they fall —

Something inhuman in you watched it all.
And whatever it is that watches,
It has kept you from loneliness like a mob.

December 8, 1989

≫ **PART ONE** ≪

Hunter in an Arctic Midnight

after Klee

He wears a sea froth of lime.
The whiskers of the walrus
say to us
that there is no wind.

The blocks of greenish ice
rise in columns
of what must be mistaken
for moonlight. The boat is made
of cured skin.

The hunter has already been forgiven.

He knows the harpoon
held waist high, parallel to the water,
is invisible to the walrus, folding
in bright triangles of blubber.

The movement from the elbow
is isosceles and serial —   one long tusk
shattering into dice
across the bluish ice that runs to snow.

The hunter's head is something of a hive,
abandoned by bees
for a lateral golden wound in a sleeping lion...

I have lied now, friends,
hoping the substitution of a glamorous cadaver
and bees from scripture

for an empty head
might preserve my walrus in his flowing sleeves.
And, yes,

I know the painting is a map of meat, ghosts
of meat.
And Klee is now dying
of a skin disease. He spies
on a winter storm beyond the stone gate.

Under morphine, he mumbles something
about the sea as afterlife, he asks for ice water,
then he dies beside the still-life
of a green enameled basin with lamp.

There were no apologies
in the elderly nurse who would soon
confess, while bathing the corpse,
that she loved the walrus above all of us.

The great pine windows rattled and shook.
Shoulders of blowing snow
pushed against the door. She knew
the far moving lights of the Solarium
were a kind of torment like large white flies.

His body was then thought to have sighed,
beyond hope, and, of course,

                                        beyond all human surmise.

A Lost Notebook of Srinivasa Ramanujan

> At Cambridge we are in darkness. No gas in the streets; few
> electric lights and those shaded; candles on the high tables.
> VICE-MASTER, TRINITY COLLEGE

> He was such a brilliant mathematician that his scrawling failures
> were as stunning as fresh marbles raised from ruin. We may be
> hundreds of years understanding the authority of just his one
> lost notebook. This sad Bengali, dead in his early thirties of
> tuberculosis, was a great visionary of the goddess of Namakkal.
> He passed, eventfully, a number of years at Trinity College. He
> died in Madras.
> BENJA R. CROOK

I.

The goddess herself rises with my fever
above the lime and apricot columns
of her cooling temple. She approaches me
with the threads of blood
my sister will arrange across the shoulders. Great

Mother will go past her temple,
down to the cremation grounds to sing.
She will lean against the white mortar
showing her genitals, a steamy
multiplying parenthesis
they will not believe back in Cambridge...

Her darkening blue husband
with a paper umbrella and bowler
is walking on the green water of the fetid
public tank—he has π
inverted as a brand on the forehead
with a coarse red line vertically through it.

9

Above his head
there were all the zeros of a Greek mathematics,
gold hoops with which to ornament
the painted seasonal elephants of the Kshatriyas:
the diseased monkeys pointing like prime numbers
to a procession of musicians
that reaches fully the colonial fort and seawall.

There are the long roots of burning dry lilies —
lepers laughing
while the Brahman's heaped banana leaf
falls to his feet. The little girl pissing in yellow grass.

When performing the arduous calculation
it rains everywhere about the house —
my fever now like a postage stamp from Bolivia.

I heard with the other boys the terrible cries
of a woman dying in childbirth. They came from a termite hill
made of bluish clay
with a poor string of dead black weeds.
The conforming symmetries of bugs
are more than inspired, I believe. The algebra of movement,
its constant,
transcribed by silent movies
was made memorable for me
by my sister carrying her basket of green nuts
out to livery.

Then the headache behind my eye: the goddess
returning as a sum of two cubes
relayed across the white rattles
now raised above the trenches
as mustard gas flows past wasted trees

into the laps
of two decapitated German sentries.

The golden mastiff barking like a hoarse jungle bird
while he lay there dying.

The temple of the deva
swells with light like a cotton wick of paraffin.
Numbers, & numbers.
It's like counting socks while compressing
a nosebleed.

The don in his gown lifting the block of ice off its straw,
then gladly the brilliant bells of my river
with the sunrise: a huge encumbered land turtle
walking out of the gates of Mother's temple
and there's no bounded error
within the dark sets of these palm trees.

But the Thames is coal black water

of a lesser multiplying murmur.
The gold hoops
now breaking in signatures above our humid heads.
The goddess is modular, consistent
like the ruined huts of rishis
scattered evenly through the dark forest
of the universe, the origin of which, dear maestro,
is so many colored toothpicks.

They want these ideas unified
beautifully in their lifetimes. *Pulp, & more pulp.*
Some poor theater
of mathematics singing back to them: no approaching field loci
in golden fractions:

the only notes that will thrive on the string
are those that exploit the dead cat
without a thought for the violin. We are all
tied off at our ends, even in death.
It's a quart of gin, a quart of turpentine,
and please pass the cotton batting.
We are living with the cosmetics of famine.

Now, again, look what I've done.
I've set them all to vibrating like the urinating fawn
who hears the approaching voices of dogs. And yes,

tuberculosis is depressing like metric tensors,
cold squash on a wooden plate, or that blonde at Cambridge
who wheeled up with her bourbon,
interrupting my meal with —
you southern Indians from Madras
are black as eels, I think,

                        kind Roger Lovelace
cracking a raw egg on her pate. I say,
no one is smart enough these days. And suddenly

it is the goddess slapping my face.

   2.

Running wickets of candles down long tables.
My friend with his hard-boiled eggs
and curry paste on crackers —
for me toast and curdled cheese.
Black brick tea from the kitchens.

With the night I dreamt of tunneling through
the cold lake —   a gold
torpedo, with Mother's sacred violet image

stamped on it—
on the bottom, predictable tall grasses

and card tables with dead men
reading their newspapers with difficulty...

The war is everywhere,

bones of lost dogs howling in zeta snow
and all those imaginary zeros dancing
for my dear friend Hardy? The frozen canals.
Logarithms of snow taking
the whole night to slow

to silence and yellow rime...
still no telegram, still no last prime.

3.

"He threw himself, unsuccessfully, before the train."
FEBRUARY 3, 1918

The consumptive insomniac of winter
interdicts sleep
exactly like that heated
black horse standing in the morning snowfall
who eternalizes crocheted ice
in wild assessments of emptying space.

4.

The midsummer full moon, blue rats
slumming in the blowing vegetal excelsior
of the monsoonal equator. Out of cremation grounds
this dripping silver aqueduct:

let the function u
whisper in the ear of its suspicious theorists:

  $u = x$ *over* $1 + x^5$

          slashes $1 + x^{10}$

              (*twixts of cane*) $1 + x^{15}$

                  vivid slashes $1 + ...$

One heavy goose and the girls with their large gourds
moving in the wind.

Cowdust falls along the ramshackle hemp
of a fence and its insepia untouchables:
Ramanujan passes a damp torn cigarette,
now 1,900 dead men
in statu khaki *pupillari...*

Their uniforms are still fresh, there's galactic polish
on the bronze buttons, and *yet*

all the boys are dead. Mother points

to the pink stylized salamander, in grotto. Or else
the S-matrix is gutless, pal. What does Herr Pagels
know of bliss? The dynamic universe
loves newsprint on its fish and chips. *The rain
has stopped for them.*

The Goddess sits in shameless rhyme
with the orange horizon —   its angry gunboats,
very much a difficult integral, the big cat
with feathers of fire,
who will not be simplified,
leaping now

through the glad starched collars
of aging professors...

In Pax Requiescat. scat, scat again.

Foolish boys, the corollary of the mother
is not the father, rather
his mother, or the barely regarded Other

which all mothers have surmised...
Now rest please, darling
dear lord Ramanujan...

Polio Season in the San Joaquin

for Nick

It was something about the mustard-colored Chevrolet
streaking along the ditch
that crosses the vineyard —   my friend, Will,
standing in the back with the blond stalk
of his grandfather's Chilean .22
putting a little elvis to the shoulder. The
rabbits lost to the zigzag dust of their stumblings
as if, one by one, they were being absorbed
into that slim margin of darkening woods.

Yet, for supper we ate pink cubes
of steak with spicy stewed tomatoes. And,

later, in the big bucket of the rusted artesian rig
Will pointed to the horizon and announced,
"The viscount of dreamless sleep? No, the marquis
of weeping":   and a huge moon rose delinquent,
barking at us.

It wasn't long before we were both up there smoking
weed and axle grease,
blinded by the light off cabbage leaves.
I was talking about a schoolgirl friend

who had drowned near the basin
in early winter.
How I had seen her in a dream —
she owned a neglected ranch
and sold jars of gin with homemade strawberry jam.
Holding the red hem of her dress, she asked

if I could shoot the two dogs
that ran down her favorite colt on Easter morning?

Nervous, I went around my father's car to open the trunk,
inside there was an eyeball of a whale
and a hundred small finless blues
snapping like mousetraps into the air —   they were all wet,
crosshatched with neon
and an occasional obscene pearl of moon.

I slammed the trunk shut and with no color in my face
said that she should ask her Portuguese uncle
to do it.
I added, the one who drove ambulances for Franco.
She giggled.

It was dark everywhere. Will said
he couldn't even think how to climb down from the rig.
I asked him to be patient.

But then the moon lost its purchase in the sky —
it fell calamitously
                              behind our conversation.

Elder Gogol's Pond at Plokhino Skete

> There is no one to read it.
> There is no one to read it.
> SAINT ELEAZOR

        Like a small yellowish waterfall
the ghost of Sophia Agapit rises from our pond. The eyes
are red and silver. Her nakedness is covered
in a green uncial script, in the perfect
hand of the other drowned nun, Xenia.

The Bolsheviks did this, first
stuffing fists of paper torn from the psalter
into their mouths. That beast
Beloborodov laughing
while drawing silk from his teeth —

he sat there shucking the corn into baskets
while judging all the river saints of our province.
Hanging them in the hermitage orchard.

He offered the czar a chair.

All the executions of Bright Week.
He laughed beside the pond.
But then his young daughter suffered
a hernia in her sleep
and died vomiting lengths of her own feces.

          ⁄€

An old woman steps out of the blowing snow.
She gestures to us.
It's as if she were scolding children.

Orange feast of the seraphim among birches.
Our dead fathers
with a moon for a trapeza. We listen now for the catechumen
of deer crossing over March ice.

>€

At a table in the darkening hall the holy father is eating
cheese and block cereal. The candle goes out.
A little wind sugaring fuses of snow
that fall from the brick tiles to white hedges.

The fasting for the Nativity is over.
Now in a cowl and stole of bright owl feathers
our martyred Batiushka-la
rises from the pink and black fumes of Moscow.

He has the river for hair, lightning for the shoelaces
they took from him before he was tortured.

Antiphons striking the sandy earth
between the Lubyianka and the poisoned river.

>€

Hieromonks walk over a steaming landscape of straw
and manure. The litia of rhubarb, beets, and cabbage.
In the cigar smoke, men laugh at the bruised shoulders
of the girl playing the piano.
The piano is our dead horse.

＞≼

Eleazar and Pascha wrap boughs of lilac
in the large pages of a newspaper. Fleas escaping.

A big trout in the sink.

＞≼

A young boy singing the first notes of Great-Saturday.
Bloodless Elijah wearing striped cuffs of pond water
crosses the supper room.
Elder Gogol
mumbles to his attendant, It will not be long now.

＞≼

Rosewater in the ledges of a baking cake. The boy asks,
"*What* will not be long now?" The sun
moving behind clouds.

Oh, *exactly* how I would put it, little one! Then, louder.
It will not be long now.

In the Palace of the Sans Souci

for Hayden Carruth

1.

Anarchists are drying the wooden forms for cheese
in an early morning sunlight
that the largest of them describes
as irredeemably bright.

His wife complains
of a taste of aspirin in the well water, she explains
that willow roots must have broken through
the green shaft's clay-brick again.

She says solemnly
that the princes' headaches will now belong to the past.
But there will be drought
and then famine following—

water leaching to the south pastures
where only stones have been harvested for centuries...

2.

But these stones are important to the *oblivio'gate*
like a groin truss at the oak pikes,
mud palisades, and the low moat
with its ferocious snapping turtles. They bob in golden flotillas
among the ornamental lilies that are almost metallic,
each shuttered like the eye of a primordial buddha's *camera
obscura...*   *ho!*

The orange excrement of turtles makes for strong lilies
that tuck to whirl-a-gig like mirroring bald plates,
all these individual faces in the one great face
of the setting sun.

There is no escaping the happiness that is outside the palace;
if you wish to question this assertion
please interview the trout.

Or the hedgehog who tells phases of the moon
to the other less significant animals

and all the woody mushrooms
like a broken choir gone searching through the tall slates
of the churchyard for a queen's blue veil

extorted by strong wind against a still shapely knee, its
long, long string of entreaty.

3.

But this queen is just an advantage of song,
a cipher,
for the princes' suffering; *her paps grew*
white and hairy!

(Their mother has been dead since the first month
of Jubilee, nearly seven years ago
this coming spring.) There was plague

even in the tenant countryside
where she did die
tormented by the seasonal crying of the many fornicating geese.

4.

But what does a drowned girl say of the flowers,
or rotting sparrowlichen —
its carrion dust poisoned the parch-flour
for the wedding cakes of princes three and eight!

So Thelma has died of the salves of rheum, coughing
phlegm and blood
onto the bibbed chest of the farmer's youngest daughter.

Why did she call out to the fens, the frozen wetlands
of *her* mother's burial: hapless,

purple processions of rue and cedar,
the great black carriage horse
suffering a clot to the brain
sliding the whole length of an incline of rotting ice
toppling hind-first
into the queen mother's grave. The walk back

was a fey lemonade poverty of handkerchiefs

and the sun broke through dark banking clouds
on the mother's daughter
blossoming now in full ovum.

5.

The anarchists are watching a large pie.

Everyone is nervous about the fat
black bee that is sampling the sweet
calluses of yellow crust. If it reaches
the deeper apple meats there will be a calamity.

Oscar, the cobbler, suggests they retreat
to shade, to drink golden mead
before they suffer any further grief?

From a windy parapet, princes one and four
are now watching their peasants
who are watching the pie. And
the princes' giggling

turns to knee slapping and then a bright shove—
was it the black bee or deep apple sills
that brought us to this crisis, prince one
screaming the whole while he was falling to the moat.

The turtles found him that night.
You can believe,
there was a gleeful feeding. The cobbler repeatedly
sighing to his wife, "No one ever listens to me."

6.

(I'm sorry but prince four cannot introduce prince one
to a turtle banquet
without raising suspicions. In fact, not without
being hung in the horse chestnut tree the very next morning
by his cruel uncles.)

The anarchists were made to witness the execution of four—
they waited till evening
and then burned their apple orchards
using pitch and lime to dry the green crying wood.

7.

These fires leapt to the park. Burning foxes
seen running to the sea. It was late.
The flames reached the oaken palace gates, the hanging tree.
This quatrain sings:

the boiling moat is soup. Four more
dead princes is eight.

8.

The anarchists are drying the wooden forms for cheese
in the late evening sunlight
that the smallest of them describes
as irredeemably white. The

wheels of cheese will be caked
in black manure. Later
a fine blue fur grows over them. Spiders leave their trash
of bright diadems. Yes, all the princes
are dead. And their saintly mother.

The anarchists are just shadows
along the warm river.

It's evening and there will be no fog.
All the silver insects
strapping on their skates.
All the night birds hovering over them. *Ate.*

Wrong Double Sonnet of the Coup d'État:

for Joaquin

The black-and-white teat mouse
is grooming his mustache
in the far orient of the coal closet.
There's paraffin and gasoline
dancing high in the trees.
Ash, small birds, and snow
falling across the luster of limousines.

Inside on the tables
there are tiger lilies in azure pots
and a manic white glove
telegraphing from the darkness.
The voice of the wind
delivering the propaganda of a winter's evening
while pronouncing,
"Yellow thumbprints
on the ballots please."

The poor who are not sick
have dragged themselves
and their children
to the strung colored lights of the plaza.

The geese flying overhead
will eliminate them with trebles
of feeling, honks,
and more coughing disdain: what of
the men and women in their high chairs
adjusting white bonnets

and bibs. Later, they will measure our fear
while testing the balcony's railing.

December 2, 2000

For the Original People

Yellow nails fall from the black night sky.
Then milk collects in the nettles.
Joe with two killing sticks and shouting
blinds the school mistress who whipped him
with the temple grass of the far Sydney basin.

A white rainbow now forms over him
just as he is shot, spun
like a barber's pole of whirlwind
into a shop's window; just
lying there in a bed of pork chops,
sausages, and veal hearts.

He's laughing at the noises in his chest—
the last, an esophageal tin whistle
that's identical to the afternoon mail,
if the old train
is climbing through monsoonal rain and hail
those last two-and-a-half miles
to the wood and watering depot.

There Joseph Nellaborr's red coffin
shimmers on its pine slurry of a platform.
The rain heavy and individual.

The original people have stopped having children.
They are being translated, plumb,
into the dark sky. Black night sky
with spent clouds.
Chalk vests of bone rising with them.
With the newest moon of no forgiving—

We have all been shunned.
There's no one to tell us about it.
It's not political. It's fish guts
festering on newspaper
behind the schoolhouse in a noon sun.
It's the maggot light of hydrogen.

We still have
our clocks, the paper money, and all
the hillside tea in China—in fact,
that's where it will begin,
much like a disease of humans,
the women drying their laundry in the trees
with the one black dog watching them intently—
his high registry of hearing now dry flax
like the old certificates of the dead

that cannot be given back.

Reading Late at Night

for the Goldensohns

I heard two women coughing
                    in the same empty room.
Watched the snow fly from the neighbor's spruce
to the roofs of the henhouses. The dog's tracks over the hill
shallow to matted timothy under the red oak.

Willa Cather wrote in some journal
that this is the woman's pleasure
in surrender...

The winter oaths are all of smoke.

The sun quietly withdraws a dark metal shank
from the ribs of the nude man
reclining on the stone wall
in that old photograph that was the foyer.

I remember the brass
of his shoulder and the hermetic sternum.

I heard a woman's voice, then another,
and smelled largely
coffee and toast.

I thought of you both.

The First Incognito

I rose from the cold bottom of the pond
with other bodies
like broken columns of numbers
on a yellow lying accountancy form —
the water was so cold that I became
more than human, unbelievably propelled
past my own air bubbles that collapse
into silver dollars as they fall back around us.

Robbed of oxygen, maybe
I was just imagining it all in some sorry tradition
like allegory.
Then again that excuse must include a huge blue and gold
coach almost resting now on the rock floor
and the confused fish who emptied himself
of a black string while swimming
through the darkening windshield
that was bigger than the swelling roadkill of elk.

I told my daughter
that I knew better than to take the all-expense-
paid promotional trip to Las Vegas. And
as I approached the broken surface of the pond
I realized that the water itself had healed into foot-thick ice —
                    rising,
I had been taken south
by spring-fed currents.

I'd read about it. This was the hell-state of a walrus.
All I could think of was my daughter, Elise,
telling me how, *to confuse the Chinese,*

the Fourteenth Dalai Lama
had said to a Western interviewer, a gentleman
named Mullin, ...*that the next time around*
he might come back as an old book,
a red ball,
or even, incognito, as an ordinary American
like Mullin himself. All of this in genuine service to all
sentient beings. But
I was thinking what if

I were this beautifully tanned Mr. Mullin
having had just another of my many audiences
with His Holiness; well, you know what I mean,
I wouldn't be that pleased being described, all of a sudden,
as just an ordinary American.
He must have been a little red in the face

while smiling all over himself, bowing, et cetera.
But I have to argue that it could have been worse —
his face going past red to blue, while tumbling back
at the bottom of a pond that was beginning actually
to look very much like a big lake, say —
the size of a Buddha's footprint. Then, then, of course,
there are the snakes —   so here we are stateline,
cropside, red flares
going down to the first buoy, the tall
fragrance of gasoline
and you want to know if I am alive —

if I was saved abstractly or something —
if I was a fatality, or, like the man said,
just one more ordinary incognito of allegory?

Boatmen on the River Mons

It was the flood that caused him
to be struck by a tree limb
just as we passed the old mud arcs
and the smell of the distant duck farms.

I made a dry compress with cobwebs
and the yellow gelatins of goat. It

draped over his eye and skull. He drank cold frog's eggs
with river from the brass spoon.

The white of the eye changed to blue.
While he died
two red hens shat, at once, scattering
the length of the packet-boat,
then trying to rise above the very ice
margins of the Mons.

Across from us in the white stand of trees:

        wattle scree, snow scree;
the magpies screaming at us both...

But I know that I am alone. In fact, wasn't that
the birds' message? I spat at them. Drank a yellow wine.
I lit heavy braids of fireworks and threw them
into the pepper and scree.
I freed the chickens and sheep and then burned the boat.

        The very sunset
deepening with my brother's fat,

old hemp, and the remaining gunpowder —
                         all of it gliding to where those birds

have nested higher from the earth than anyone can remember.

But with my brother, they will now adjust their calculations
beyond oblivion to the glamorous silting
of the trapezium in Orion...
It reflects off the river bottom, across the rain barrels
of our small town
to the open grave we'll decorate
tomorrow with long green ribbons,
wet chrysanthemums, and a burning sow.

Nightmare with Heat Lightning

for Marcel

She stood cold and straight in a red circle of anthills.

The garments floating under the water,
under a dark slough of jade,
are in fact short jerseys of algae
crazily made by the hungry eyes of alligators and snakes.
The legs are young willow

bleached by the July exhaust
of the storm-flooded salt marsh.
She screams at seeing the children
folded like flags in the back channel
of a darkening glade.

What surprised her in this dream
was the way an illicit dirt
clothed her lost children, and the way
slurries of clay
from a spade once paved
her dead daughters' grave for the rumpled cat-killed blue jay.

The Young Professor from Wyoming Wears a Red-Banded Skin of Snake on the Spirit Finger of Her Right Hand That Shakes...

for Lukeon

I.

We will not speak of these snowy Hopi orchards again.
Though, the snow has been falling here for hours
and I have seen the red tree
with ribbons of green and yellow crepe
draping the large Even Woman...

Her eyes and the many dry rooms of her rattle
are not aligned
so as a coiled snake she is a poor
artifact of spiral...

In a cave of snow there are two sacred heaps:
one of orange needles from the pine meadows
and the other:
yellow teeth of the javelinas
who were fed hearts of agave all spring.

The poles of Earth are not plumb either,
just like the chalk stars in constellation
over a gopher snake. So a bit of pencil
rising with an opposed but feathered spin
will inscribe a failed circle
that is the mother-spiral's naked relative,

or adage.

2.

The extremes of the tree, north and south,
follow the circumference of the circle
that the fragment of spiral
impatiently classifies as Earth's wobble.
Its limits are, by example, the furthest reaches of desire
the spiral can overcome.

So he is thinking of his lover
while she is in Manhattan
suffering from the last
of her inoculations before traveling to China.

Snowburned, shy in his long hair,
crossing through mountains
on the spotted ruin of a donkey, he clears her mind
with a quick telegraph
of erasure and elation. Then, in fever,
she clears even her memory of dinosaurs,
of the wind kneeling in pines.

The bones of her dead climb like escalators of stone —
he feels delayed by a simple mathematics, the idealized
rooms.

He gawks at the barest breast
of this ghost of an orchard woman, sits,
and writes,
in a manner desperate and propelled,
that the tropics of geometry are a drug like love itself.

3.

Sleeping at Walpi, he dreams that black sheep
are shitting green wafers into the mesquite.

So, he thinks, sometimes the wind must even
suffer itself —   all the glassy obloquies
of his grandmother's collapsed aluminum shack.

In the milk-drawn hallways of serial agates
one naked light is enough.
Not like the match tossed into straw, more
like fruit
turned to ornament, crosshatched
with the lacquer of darkness. (*The yellow postcard
from China.*) Or baffles of longsheep
eating the paints off the desert floor.

The reddish fallen cactus
is a dead man's pajamas.

When the wind is this empty, she thinks
it's no longer just a salt passage from night
to day, or day to night. It is
the sigh that uncovers a breast,
the breast that barely covers a lie.

4.

Or is it a planet traversing the teal dunes,
a white dry cache of eggs, the blind
cook with the reflection of the moon
for a face. She has eaten again
the dry potatoes and onions with sausages. *I scribbled*

a speech about the Sun as objective
datum. The wind tips the cook's jeep.

This storm off the Gobi
reaches for their documents,
the fat
gray and turquoise stamps
from the last Chinese depot
with lepers

kneeling across from them
in what's been a long journey.
The youngest of them shows her neck,
her cigarette holder is the green fang
of a giant anaconda with the brown stub
of a Russian cigarette,
the blood of her hand quickly drying on it.

The wind, I wrote, is so strong
that my stunned tent stands like the filament
inside the one lamp.

This wind buries three children and a fishing shack
in North Korea. It sands and then paints
the collapsed Baptist clerestory and melon stand
on a lesser island of Micronesia. It makes
the cow dry and faint.

It raises then a great page of newsprint, slapping
it against a bedroom window, in Gallup,
New Mexico.

This stops the hundred-
syllable prayer
because the wind has recognized its husband: old sticks

and the crushed wing of a chalk kiva,
north and easterly —   no celery,
we have eaten potatoes with sausage for days.

Lizards with sails are
screaming to her while the green spade
opens a whole nursery, a powdered vault of spotted dinosaur eggs
racked in loose hexes of eight,

and a black wind traverses the dunes. Or
a planet traverses that wind: its
lost fisher-children,
and powder sortilege of eggs.

The woman with the cigarette saying,
when it reaches the Americas
it will take the sun away for three days.

The Winter Apocalypse of Doctor Caleb Minus

It's nothing to do with the Elders,
in Holland, smelling of figs. It's not a quaint fire?

But the Daniel tract points
clearly to an age of steam that has passed us.
Yet, what if,
in that old flux of the locomotive's woodbox

something conical and atomistic
began to rotate and stack in open arrays
of the figure eight —   then projecting the good doktor
through time and space?

In what quarter of Jerusalem
will the moon rise from its resin bath?

Burning palms all resting at failed angles
to the earth. The red-haired
child carefully crossing the walk
with two waxpaper cones
spilling raw cow's milk.

I might add, sideways to the treatise on steam,
that some dark riverboat gambler
has dressed an affluent evangelist in diamonds
where he stands
sensing a rival in the gymnasium's old pommel horse,
dressed in what he's mistaken
for an obvious Egyptian body rag, rather attractive
to the evangelist —
especially through the collapsed diaphragm and ribcage.

The children down from the mountain
begin to giggle at him.

The real humiliation is
there's no agreement about the year:
some say "odd-two" or "six," there's "eleven,"
or possibly even "thirteen." "Like a thief in the night"
is how we think of it. Ah yes, raisins
in the eggnog please. Snow falling on hedgerows.
Lola peering into her cup says, "How do you know
they aren't mouse turds?"

Finally tiers of paraffin dancing in the chandeliers.

It's difficult concentrating on the old technology
of steam. Yet it's where all the prophets bring me:

Old wine and circulating triangles of cucumber sandwich
with a very rich mayonnaise. *Friends,*
it's significant, if not imminent. And

we must say interesting, how the wind
has morphed together, made mundane,
all the burning trees. Mundanized the scene, *as it were.*
Or maybe?

Unbelievably serene —   the poet now
volleys to Lola: *fuck 'em,*
I never trusted these people anyways.

Taos

January 3, 1943

You threw the red and white saddle blanket
into the black berth
and sat cross-legged for hours
in the sleeping car
of the mile-long silver train to Los Angeles.

Snow over the fields of cactus was moonlight, you thought —
walls of piñon and sandstone with liver spots
of raw orange and pitch
like that chunk of uranium you left on your aunt's
sewing machine the night before Easter.

Your cigarette flares against glass. You open
the thermos of hot chocolate and brandy:
a week ago
your mother had died in her sleep

so now you must remain awake
thinking the white rails of the mountain roadbed
are climbing vertically to the vanishing point
like your narrowing scream
        in the unwanted winter midnight.

➤ PART TWO ⬿

...let all true sympathizers come,
Without the inventions of sorrow or the sob
Beyond invention.
STEVENS

Whose instructions made the yellow
arrow straight, the fletcher's or the sun's?
My conclusion knows the archer is the one.
ECKHART

Shambhala

a dream fragment

I.

The Oleshe Lama staggers back from his fire,
a sooty mucus and milk in his mustache.
His rosary is an avalanche of pepper
and sheared cedar boughs:
folds of snow blowing shadows
before the North Star; lifting
his pearl astrolabe at angles
to the sparkling horizon, he screams:
it is the sun at noon — and
he believes...

The Chinese bearer thinks he's been eating
the roast of his forearm, writs
of gangrene
having nibbled at it in the morning.

The white limb cauterizes in the peach blood
of a fresh snow.

Longitude is just Time, the seconds
of which arrive
like yeti footprints. Latitude is
the broken back of a yak buffalo
that Tibetans worship
at the gates to the underworld. Dead yak,
but with legs spindled in rainbows and gold braid,
still convulsing in the full cataract

of an old moon lake, not
the Issyk Kul.

yama toko, ya mantaka, phat.

2.

Our bleached tents are yellowing again, membranous
with the quicklime of a shifting wind
like the foul sinuses of a camel
kneeling now for days in the blizzard.

We dream of a city of bells, or
of madder lakes with lines
of sky-iron inching away
into the hillside mustard beyond Kashmir.

Then another plague of windlike metallic insects
swarming over the eyes of the tormented horses —
one jumps off the cliff, plunging — no,
floating like its eyeballs above the distant glacier.

The Oleshe Lama says that the horse's
crazed brain
allows him to perceive the glacier
as rising to envelop him —   perfect
sphere of sky and snow, a bit of pork
in dough, but glassy, reflective — actually,
just a big eyeball suffering the attraction
of an even larger sphere, not exactly
unknown to us.
He is driving me mad with these wisdoms.

I point to tell him: look, the horse
is being dragged away by the garrison's soldiers;

they'll eat it with a live spring rice
and biscuit.

3.
circa 2379 c.e.

The gray hooded figures
have been with us for two days—
a naked Arab woman, arms
bound behind her in rope, closely
follows. She holds

a fat strawberry between her teeth.
If she swallows it, the first groom
to the camels will behead her in the morning,
before their prayers and tea.

In the sky the vultures are like a dark lace canopy
sheltering the barbarians
from broad bands of ultraviolet rays.

We have gone beyond
the last barrier of mountains, Charlus Nuur,
the poisoned waters of an ack-dorge, patches
of desert and now the outer stairs
of the ice city. The Tashi Lama is sky,
hides behind trees...

The Slam-barbarian jets
with laser sequence spears are shooting,
not at the King, but at his wild
double envelopment of mantras
like barbers' ladders in lotus tiers
around him.

The blue smoke
from the underground library swirls with morning fog.
Lords of Shambhala
laughing at the barbarians' quick copy wedge
of airships.

om ha swa ha ksha, mala vara yam.

4.

> There are so many errors on the maps.
> There are maps on maps.
> NICHOLAS ROERICH

The craters from their bombs are changing
into the Buddha's footsteps,
his mother's arms
snaking into green tree limbs
where she has just given birth to him.

In weeks, she'll be
dead of a septic trench to the stomach —
white bats
dropping rosewater cakes for the funeral guests

who are admiring the infant's
voluble watery syllables
released with an instinct
more of laughter
than of eventful sentences.

The sun sets on the 4 o'clock petal
of a darkening mandala that is the city.

5.

Barbarians swarm over the North Pass.

The hooded men have in their sleep
loosened the ropes on the Arab prisoner.
She is blue with the cold, between
her teeth is the fat human heart of that day
with white hair and facets of a wild fruit.

It is the Nairatmya Buddha
and she sweeps
with a scythe through the high
blue and gold collars of their mounted militia.

She flies to a rooftop, breaking the necks
on their fallen elephants.
Her compassion is limitless.

At her feet, a thousand butter daisies growing
between tiles.
The enemy dead are dragging large shoes of coal
into the noon kitchens. From inland a great wall of water
falls on Beijing.

It straightens like the hair of a dead woman.
The visceral rope of yellowing ibis draped from pole to pole,
the ghost wind-horse
screaming to the mother of Shambhala.

France now dying of radiation. And the land
moved out and away from the Mississippi,
one whole night – the river entirely swallowed
by the earth – steam rising in the dark sky,
boiling thousands of square miles of corn
still standing in fields.

Damascus is a plain of glass.

A thousand butter lamps float over the Manjushri Khit.

The daughters of the barbarian king
carry their dead father to the underworld
where the cattle god now stands on him.

Our dead king is being born again
in the pink watery lens of a flowering lotus.
Cosmological warships lift and leave the long spine
of the smoking peninsula. The Gobi sits like a pond
beneath us.

It was said that one day they would wipe
their brows with black cloths.
They would wrap sticks of dynamite to the necks
and ankles of the great stone Buddhas.

We knew that they would not return for very long
to their poppies.

The poppies that grow milky
like the blind eyes of their wizard children.

6.

for Heather

An artesian water-gig volunteering in the evening's mustard:
the dustfall of cowflies, stooped
and complicated by light—

small girls in yellow rags are
leaving the thousand years of a dry hillside;
the earth moves

lifting the children into sky,
to the poor kitchens of the darkening mountain
where hungry birds in their least bright aspect
                                        reply
in generous laughter-like repetitions of flight...
it is again
            the mother night.

The Pit

Each green leaf on the ginkgo tree
is caked like a tongue
with the flash milks of magnesium.

There are many of these trees.

So the cavity of sky above them
speaks, when it does,
with a thousand tongues.

Not *la-la-la,*

but not sad, either.

A heavy sewn ball from the cooling gymnasium
flies past helmeted firemen
who are cleaning the tongues of the ginkgo,
first of all allegory,
and then of tedium. It was an academic exhaustion
that left filth on the tongue of the ginkgo. It is
always like this —

for instance, in a moment of early photography,
the nude Parisian woman
tosses a leather ball above her head,
lengths of hair cascading
over the breast with its quarter-moon scar
and three lesser moons
that are its companions.

The photographer under his black cloth
is asking himself
if the streetwalker's toppling auburn hair
somehow increases the importance of his composition.

She giggles, he thinks, unreasonably,
like a ginkgo tree —   all of its tongues
touching all of its teeth.

The yellow salts of the darkroom baths,
he suspects, have made him mad.

The Ottoman Empire has collapsed.

His widowed mother becomes a refugee to France.
Their September picnics are always situated here,
precariously, under the ginkgo trees —

ash from furnaces, ashes
from the twin stacks of a nearby iron foundry
color the ginkgo

the broad violets of a reflected evening light
that rises off the silent river
while their napkins are gathered up
with red lengths of river water
into the straw basket of a dead grandmother.

These conflagrations of skyline
announce the night
like a pit beside a river
from which Professor Tropielle excavated
a stone weapon and the hairless newborn mammoth

from the very last of the great mass extinctions.

Winter Garrison

In Afghanistan, women are turning
in bright reckless arcs of atmosphere,
starlight sweeping gun-post and jeep chrome
through the dark hill station —   distanced
from one another and from us
they are turning along the mountainside,
weighted in lengths of abundant moon,
dragging hems of turnip skin
from the clay combs of a grandfather's root cellar.

They are the poorly sewn flags of obvious memory.

Once, I sold them contaminated powders of biscuit
and milk —
for who else would want it —

it's like

extracting two black teeth

from the head of a dead donkey.

The tallest had tossed shocks
of blue thistle into a banked fire
and her sister now
speaks to a fallen marine, just a schoolboy,

from Rome, N.Y. —
the numerary voices of a single sentence
forming,

Look above you, above the dunes, to the dark caves:

there our dead husbands, motionless
in winter shirts, are fasting;
they are

round tufted pullets of oxen fat and snow...

Below the gold tinfoil of satellites,
the locust walked onto the land

all along the Bengali coast;

like big tacks in the moonlight
they allow the long arroyos to cling to a planet
that is turning dry on a dry cedar post...

The Pasha on the Hill

I'm told that someone runs ahead of us
with the messages.

Afflicted by dream,
the Pasha sleeps on his golden balcony
where on cold evenings the torch
above him sings to the ice
of all the comforting yellows
in a blossoming acacia field
that moves like the horizon
just beyond a doubtful paradise.

Now that everyone suffers,
even the practice of torturing prisoners
seems the highest immutable kindness.

Two bushes beside the road to the iron rigs
burn like the acacia without smudging.
The women
hanging in the orchards
have, without ceremony, healed themselves
of hunger and anxiety.

A young widow's distant lamp
walks out to her chickens and peahens —
she follows in the dark
like brilliant inclines of cascading salt...

I fear
that I will bore you with so much pain
and the consequences are real —

the conscience of the tenement
confesses that my happiness was never spontaneous.

The last of the phantoms
descends to the sea, saying
in her own voice, in columns
of imagery like written Chinese, that
red and gold laments have defeated
hunger in the belly, that unbelievably
government has made the cruelest of religious promenades
seem innocent like snow on a leaf.

I could not have thought of these things for myself,
but, friends, please,
in the dizzying June heat of my servant's torch, believe
I may not find my mouth. I may not
find the heart to hope for the more perfect misery.

Blue

In that first harsh winter of the war
I dreamt a great pear of a man, sun-ripened
in red cotton
and greenish brocade, on the twenty-sixth night
of a not very difficult fast, was
presenting to me thirty-two
separate gifts of gold.

Each carried a fragment of verse.
The first was pure and formal, but the test,
on this blue night of *sohbet,*
was to make his remaining offerings
increasingly vulgar,
more the desperate prayers of a sincere blasphemer?

There was something here of the burden of a life
and the breathless exercise of stairs.

For the dying *mevlana*
there was the admonition of his lover
not to count the heavy kisses
falling like coins onto his beard; not
to count the counting, as with the days,
rising integers of nothing,
going nowhere; just

look upon him
in simple praise of what it is that increases
for *that* is exactly what will, in secret,

be taken away.

Intolerance

The grass fires were isolated from the rosy morning
by the daily mowing
down the switchbacked limestone paths
that have kept these volcanic grasses
from the narrow petrol ponds since, well,
the earliest work on the Pontine marshes...

The lawyer's house has a lovely turquoise shelf
of algae
that runs from a leaky air conditioner
to the bedroom window
where the dying Vatican secretary slept
under checked blankets on the old willow chaise.

He was senile like a parrot.

When he
suffered a nosebleed, he'd stick
his head out the window,
blood splattering on the calla lilies,
screaming always at a female officer
in a white blouse
who directs traffic at this quiet Roman intersection.

The yew tree there was painted white
and the sun climbs just beyond it.
The apocalypse of grasses was just down the hill,
west of our marshes.

I was cleaning straw from the fountain
when a flock of birds flew overhead

confirming a need to read the Mahabharata
with bowls of fresh cream and fiber.
The yellow honey
from the south was for the black biscuits.

Of course it was the priest's nosebleed
that sent the burning carts
down into the drier grasses.
The patient children from the tenements
would have waited weeks
before tossing their stick matches into it.

I missed the collision
while looking up at that strange alphabet
of migratory birds,
thinking my wife's sex
once relayed the cool alcohol breath
of *slivovitz* from me to the greater world.

I did see the officer
remove her blouse, making a tourniquet
that she tightened around an old woman's leg.

The old woman cursing, to my surprise,
in German. No longer a doctor,

I crossed over
offering my services as her translator,
my wife later
adding for our sons, *he was studying no doubt
the officer's resolve and respiration?*
Secretly, I believe, we are all possessed

with patience like a cow. Blood
still falling

a full twenty-five paces to the waiting calla lilies —
their mouths are open also, saying,

                              Jesus,

if you can, save us now?

Ordinary Mornings of a Coliseum

Please, not that rustling in the grass again...
H.D.

I.

The dull straightedge and a dab of chicken fat,
I was shaving in a fragment of mirror glass,
the rising sun crowning my bare shoulders. Asleep,

you dreamt the overhanging rainbow of saltimbanques —
then, the checks of black and white: or,
an ivory alphabet of the dead, levitated:

> *He was hanging at his knees from the high branch*
> *of a dark tree. His cape*
> *quickly brushing against her hair and face; also naked,*
> *she sat there on a large black horse, its nostrils*
> *expressing a scalded milk.*
>
> *So, just a moonless sky, the clair silhouette*
> *of two hairless bodies*
> *seemingly unrelated in the enveloping night.*
> *We are confessing again to the morning*
> *and its shaded sparrowhawk,*
>
> *I killed the lovers with your yellow arrows.*
> *The rain washing their blood from the noble horse.*
> *The rising sun*
> *driving them back into their white paper costumes.*

Now the sky paraclete, Moloiel, writes in his history
that the traces of iron and sulfur in oxblood

will someday motion like knives
erasing the flooding atoms of ink to parchment.

We think the pigeons around the coliseum
are thrilled with the sputtering pink
orchids of diesel. These days,

there are fewer semicolons in judgment.

Just a large red wall, some white bones
behind it; here is
the room of sighs and the laughter
of what is called "the graveyard."

The Vatican telegraphing
a rural priest who said water gushed from living stone
and seemed to possess the feral powers
of our Mother's tears *themselves.*

The priest washed his turned knee in the grotto's pool. Below him
a procession of masons leaving the morning meal
to bathe in the cold river.

She walked past us – draped over her head a beige altar cloth
with its delicate gold ancestry.

The horse still idling in rain.

*In your sleep you murdered
the little renault and that spirit above her, two
ciphers of the gothic copse, using
the old poisoned arrows of the coliseum. Blackbirds
scavenging across the high mead tables.* Off

on our green hill, you saw the details
of an enumerated intaglio: Sixtus IV
admiring

                              the small blue observatory
and the newly constructed basilica squatting like a greening toad
in that smoke that we mistook for fog…

And later the painters of the Renaissance pressing kerosene
from tubs of pitch. Flocks of birds
climbing above the fields of red wheat
and the narrowing margins of boxwood bleeding
significance?

    2.

The paraclete in his oaken slipper is on the canal,
black velvet pillows
and the chuck-burning pipe of opium. A small boy is
paring the prelate's toenails, fresh oranges, snails —
even the blue-silver ramshackle
of the constellation *Croix de Guerre*
climbing on the moldering horizon —

the red coral domination of the sun
rebukes the hand mirror
in which the metropolitan Moloiel watches
across his cheek
the migrating white mole with a red hair in it.

Why would he poison this sick old pontiff
who'll be dead by midsummer?

You thought it was his saltimbanques and lapdogs
that woke you, but
it was the breathing of the older men

with long scythes
mowing the cool dewy floor of the coliseum.

3.

M. bathes your chest in witch hazel from a tin cup,
and your fever plummets
with the song of the sparrowhawks...

The sky priest would comfort you with a bath
of green talc. *We are this triangle of men.*

Alewives swimming from the nostrils,
cicadas sounding in the advocate's canal of the right ear,
rheum lineaments touched
to the back of the politics of illness
that is becoming you.

Your strict friends sway, first in an ocean
of ovation, and then in the lesser blood channels of the cats
while a large female tiger
casually circumambulates, drags
the dead deserter about by a glistening
knot of tendon with bluish muscle.

For this moment, Jackal, these collapsing saltimbanques of color
are just the tall phenomenon of rain
and that rain's secret protocol...   Moloiel

pouring the dust of gold over balancing pans.

4.

The mosquitoes jumping now with the late hour
and I can hear
lions coughing below the pilasters.

They are scattering after fat cockroaches
over the limestone benches. Desperate, starved,

this winter they burrowed down into the catacombs
gnawing at the spun bones
of mummified Christians. These damn bureaucrats
would refuse soup to their mothers. Peter climbing
like an arrangement of chalk, pounding
from his side of the red wall
while curlews of silt fall from his hair and shoulders.

Caesar, who
loves these big cats, and all atmospheres of dejection,
walks off with a retinue
of lamps and virgins. *It is the day of the Ten.*

5.
    for Chris

                        The sick painter in a yellow bonnet
looks up while a meteor crosses the heavens, crashing
beyond the green hill. A figure of wet white smoke
seems almost spoken by the chimney. He worked so long

on his scaffolding, that he must
sit now in a tepid tub to separate
caked blood from his leather apron and trousers.

M. reminds us of the girl who was your mother.

Rome, in these leaf fires, is inscribable. It is
an Easter for bureaucrats and the half-dressed working women
of our avuncular palazzo and its pigeons.
They carry the dead by on litters. Torches

run from the city to the sea. I smell the approaching war cart
filled with fresh garlic. I wish
the ridicule that fell on the priest in the grotto
would come here and fall upon me. I wish this priest
in his torn work shirt would come and bathe me
in pungent spirits, the long cool alcohols
of cat piss tossed with straw. I wish, Caesar, you

would go wash yourself in the offals of the hour.
We are following a hunger of tigers
                                        into some era of lost protocol:
As we fall, an ether falls with quick indulgences of pearl.

     6.

I've admired the half-eaten pear
on the high mud shelf.
M. is drafting again at the table.

Without the matted brick of grasses
the trout would be cooked on dung—
elephant, tiger, even dog at one senator's
summerhouse? But
he had passed, of course, years
on the Nile.

There was a stabbing last night
at the open-air cinema...   Sicilian women
with brooms, who mistook the victim
for the villain, crushing his ribcage and skull.

There were more falling stars! The radical Indogen
Eckhart smiles...

I can covet a certain gown on a priest.
The pope, though,
seems to be a snow-laden tree to me.
Yes, a conifer.
We are now visualizing conifers,
a whole parking lot full of them —
in Paris, sad with one thin string of colored lights.

The Vatican secretary, putting aside his sacks of gold, walks
out into the cold sunlight
to feed individual leafs of lettuce to the browning of caged hares.

When the coliseum floors are excavated there are still
the running smells
of punk ozone, urine,
and the rotting roses of old iron.
The blood petals on the centurion's bare shoulder fall at last
to the mildewed straw.

Mother of God,
                    there are further semicolons
in judgment? Sentences eschewing sentences?

The Moloiel bathing giant carp in waters of vinegar...

7.
       circa 1473

We are struggling now, Jackal, to name you.

Unable to sleep, listening to the cries
of the millennial lion...   what naked boy
did they share in this cometary garden light?

The papal secretary is gathering the sage of Corfu
into the milliner's sling that is over his shoulder.

The goats eating limestone above him
make a study of a long formation of blackbirds
arriving in North Korea the next morning.

Kore, where else, in hell with the boiling eels?

All the gold ponds of the tannery, like those coins
M. raked from the fountain
that the giraffe had urinated in,
early January...   white ibis

now just climbing off the surface
of the watery terraces at Assisi.

The purple mackerel in its mouth
is not, *he says,*
the illusive mustache on the false pope to come

who, twice each day since childhood, has
shaved himself with a pat of chicken fat
and the full Sanskrit edge of a clamshell.

At Corfu

for Beckian

In seventeen hundred, a much-hated sultan
visited us twice, finally
dying of headaches in the south harbor.

Ever since, visitors have come to the island.
They bring their dogs and children.

The ferryboat with a red cross
freshly painted on it
lifts in uneven drafts of smoke and steam
devising a mustard horizon
that is grotesque with purple thunderheads.

In the wind the angry seabirds
circle the trafficking winter ghosts
who are electric like the locusts at Patmos.

They are gathering sage in improvised slings
along the hillsides,
they are the lightning strikes scattering wild cats
from the boneyard:
here, since the war, fertilizer trucks
have idled much like the island itself.

We blame these feral cats who have eaten
all the jeweled yellow snakes.

When sufficiently distant, the outhouses have a sweetness
like frankincense.

A darker congregation, we think the last days
began when they stripped the postage stamps
of their lies and romance.

The chaff of the hillsides
rises like a cramp, defeating a paring of moon...   its
hot, modest conjunction of planets...

And with this sudden hard rain
the bells on the ferryboat
begin a long elicit angelus.

Two small Turkish boys run out into the storm —
here, by superstition,
they must plow and sing
like condemned lovers who are ashen and kneeling,
being washed
by their dead grandmothers'
grandmothers.

Death by Compass

We are scrolling between rims of glass,
a cold sweat
on Rimbaud's radical carafe of tea
made with the skin of yellow African herbs,
gunpowder, and a bright urine
falling from his tall black nurse
through a fine filter of green chemise
while the August sun climbs above a banana grove
with its white skirt of pepper trees.
In this long dream of Shoa
the nurse said to his young sister,
in her straw hat,
that he was dead
of a blood poisoning to the leg:

                              a long dream, to be exact,
                              of that very afternoon
when cold black manure was being spread
over most of the open pasturage, in France.

So, what do you think?

Book Title: ....

Comments: ....

....

....

....

....

Can we quote you on that? ☐ yes ☐ no

Copper Canyon Press seeks to build the awareness of, appreciation of, and audience for a wide range of emerging and established American poets, as well as poetry in translation from many of the world's cultures, classical and contemporary. To receive our catalog, send us this postage-paid card or email your contact information to poetry@coppercanyonpress.org

NAME: ....

ADDRESS: ....

CITY: ....

STATE: .... ZIP: ....

EMAIL: ....

COPPER
CANYON
PRESS

www.coppercanyonpress.org

BUSINESS REPLY MAIL

FIRST-CLASS MAIL   PERMIT NO. 43   PORT TOWNSEND WA

POSTAGE WILL BE PAID BY ADDRESSEE

Copper Canyon Press
Post Office Box 271
Port Townsend, WA   98368-9931

The Desert Census of Elder Cyril, the Little Hermit of Antioch

I.

He mistook me in a hot sun
for the Holy Virgin, undressed
and climbing up from the river
to greet him — he thought my buttocks
were rhyming with the haunches of a black mule
that the Virgin hurried with her white branch
past the cold pond
rank with cadaver.

He said there were the fadings of a geometry
and red tattoos everywhere
on her body while she flew above the orchards.

He's become, mostly in his mind,
radiant with the olive trees and re-dacted palms.
A poor traveler escorting a live star
with washboard margins
of gravity that serve him as a lens,
that will straighten even the purple tongue

of a morning's burden that he has shunned:
the still-fresh corpse of the water-bearer's daughter
who, in kindness, I must speak of
as the legitimate child
of a long shyness of trees.

She's the actual seed of the last surviving Elder,
Cyril's old friend, Octavio. She *is*

the last surviving member of a garden community
of desert fathers —   for

Cyril, I must explain,
doesn't count himself *extant,* not even among the feral cats —
save one, the Memphis kitten
of mixed blood
whom he christens both *Zero* and *Song.*

Later, in the worst weather,
which always begins with a moving cursive wall of sand,
he'll think this cat
just a figment of his loneliness,
made of spoiled rice, and amber crystals of scrolled honey:

an offering to Mary, which a fact of cats
gobbles up before the rare orange cock
accuses the cat of being an accomplice
to the rising sun, sending him
straight into the arms of the sleeping hermit.

Lord, Cyril comments, a startled figment of cat
just woke me from my nap.
Avalanche of dander absorbing my wonderment and tears
at knowing, now, I'm not alone. Alien, yellow

dander clouding this dragon, Zero,
in a shared waking shock that might
some day empty the dark tombs
on the distant hillside...

The passing traders' cock and camels
continue their ferocious barking at Matins.
The bones of the water-bearer's daughter
mime his empty stomach.

Lord, I'd have buried the child
and the innocent viper that bit her
out there by our pond,
but all these deaths of the past eleven months
seem unlikely, illusory
while I've competed with the moon for wet black plums.

Octavio said the girl's
first thought about the venom
was slower than the venom itself.

I croaked, yes, and the Holy Mother is like that, friend...

Both laugh, rising above a dark ramshackle desert.

2.

in memoriam, Susan Morrill, 1954–2002

I can't believe it, Lord.
Your locked servant is undone
by the mere amorous snoring of a kitten.
Elder Octavio, much smarter than I, mused,
"All human curiosity is horseshit!"

So the girl's body beside the water also seems,
in this heat and ecstasy,
to be some pharaoh's throne of angry bees.

There were the bronzed, crossed sticks
or yoke of Moses, couch
for the serpent who is our starry night, a cosmic lord
blinding to the fleeing Israelites
whose ankles were being stung by faster, whiter serpents —
the minions, belly bright and difficult.

A gulping night's drought has brought
crocodiles with raw carbuncle snouts
up to the pond and windmill —   they dragged
the child's corpse into the river's green waters,
her head
thrashing as if in some repeated questioning.

Then she vanished in it all.

Stars
like pain, fangs of a snake
in the pearl of her ankle,
the fallen water-bearer
and now her child
like new constellations in a night sky
just beyond the Nile.

The merchants
from Cathay at their banked fires
across these hills
sound like lost Elders disputing, *first*
the radishes in the volunteering garden,
then the coughing in the celery stalks. The whisk

made from a plait of mule hair kills the fat
emerald fly who was inching over the table.

He was a spiritual scribble of cattle dust
in the vacant sky.

The propane ghost
of the dead girl weaves through the broken permission
of trees where caterpillars are boxing rainbows
before the burning hair of a new moon.

3.

for Chris

Lord, it's the long devotions that make
of me a poor carrier of corpses. Those instructions, it seems,
have properly reached the crocodile, lion, and crow.

The cat, Zero,
shits a whole alphabet of mice bones
with no trouble — *what am I to think, Lord,*
dreaming of the whores of Alexandria
bathing my rotten foot with herb waters and lamb's wool,
their breasts shifting in the yellow river.

Zero laughs at the holy man
and then laps away at souring goat's milk
that moves in the halved black skull of a camel.

He, the cat, is in a reverie of past life
remembering some stanzas written on a winter night
with dogs barking in the long alley.

It is the restless sleep of a last day
with a vision
of the flattened clavicle and its rouge —
the eyes closing on its own beheading.

Just these facts, and a yellow and black
Memphis cat called Song...

The purple marrow of a dyed flax
over in the slave's shack. Moon-cooled lathe of river clay
rising with sun-waxed apricots.

Lord, the rains
have become the hissing rhetoric of rats
quarreling in the open grain barges.
Among their cries I found red fragments of a sickly
dog who was overwhelmed,
who spoke with the locust, saying,

"I am undone, I am no one. It is the thunder of perfect
mind, repeating that we were baptized
in waters of darkness, beyond
the veils of time, beyond
even the women preparing themselves for their new husbands.
The lamps spending light on them
in ten directions."

4.

The clear paste, ray-feathers of cranes, the soft
almost sanded skin of them, thin
as paraffin set with muslin.
They are the door to my spiritual cabinet.

The confused rain, Lord, is just
more sand striking the cool shellac
of these winged dead things
over the dark narrow opening to my cave.

What of the havoc of a stone rolled back.

The solitary and guiltless undead are everywhere.
It's why I refused them graves.
These sepia ghosts in foul linen
must arrange themselves at the table,
praising this meat dish with berries,
that perfect tangerine,

and the weak tea
of our seminary days.

Lord, we think it is thee
who is eating me!

    5.

I was bringing the heavily salted briskets
down from Cairo to the seven towns.

I went to visit my friends,
the old desert hermits.

I found them all dead
and then, past midnight, I saw the ghost of little Cyril
in the larger orbit of his own ghosts. He pointed
saying that they *were* the ghosts of noon.

He then spoke, unreliably, about their end days.

I don't know where I found the courage,
but I looked straight into his eyes,
milk opals from the burning bismuth mines,
his arms open with sores, and

I said, "Father, beloved one,
I sometimes wonder
if it wouldn't be less trouble
having an obvious god,
stair in a storm rowing,
the seated human night with fists, 90 degrees,
black copper and turquoise eyes from floor to ceiling,
just bowing to its light,

a louvered light welcoming a rain of milk,
that sets to simmering
a grandmother's sweet phyllo cream.

What I am proposing, Father, might be
the simple ignorant dream
I have of a white bearded ox
who pulls my carts from Jerusalem
to Damascus, from a burning Damascus
to Cairo.

In fact, from equinox to equinox. Then back, again,
to Jerusalem, its gold domes burning also, smoke
and fog blanketing the city
like a wormy sack thrown over the shoulders
of an old black mule
distancing his weeping sores
            from the weeping of the mule."

The Pendulum

after Philip K. Dick

Though not human, the dead language of the insect
is Latin. I've martyred myself here
in their suburbs so as to observe them.
No, not the insects, Martha.

The mowed lawn under a cold rain
though, is breathtaking. It is the odor
of a tall flowering
bean-guano on our planet—   its brilliant
waistcoat of azure tar. A neurotic
plant, one ate our sister the very day of my birth.

Understood as very meaningful,
it was our sister's unlikely death
that found me shunned, sent
to this Earth as a witness
with none of the Messenger's privileges.

It is a hell state, Martha.

By contrast, our older brother, Guillaume Postel,
brought the first Coptic alphabet
to France. He was showered with gifts
like the one-eyed bureaucrats of Lyra.

By example, when the cousin, Messenger Frumence,
died at the age of 118,
he was living
among the desert fathers of Wadi Natrun.
Two lions, smoke- and honey-colored,

dug furiously for much of the winter night
so the Saint Messenger would enjoy
a burial before first light.

Or, Saint Jerome
once was fed chunks of very red watermelon
by large crows that were garrulous.

But, Martha, I will die at fifty-four.
In a barbarous township
of late-twentieth-century North America.
A Thorazine drip
backing up into my blue shoulder.
Some dull white-haired nurse
will not report how she lost
a rectal thermometer
deep within my bowels.

They believe in little, but are oddly heroic.
They will eliminate themselves, save two
communities in Ethiopia, through the manufacture of toxins:
weaponry, agriculture, energy,
medicine, and a class of plastics
that is the only unique product of their global culture.

This cynical vegetal psyche
overwhelms me.

But they do have something
that resembles our moonrise
they call music. I'm often transfixed by it. Yes,
Martha, they do, as you say, resemble giraffes
in the very way that a brick
resembles an egg.

I do envy you your solitudes.

It has added something very precise
to your speculations about life
in all its forms. Tell Father
that feeding the blue grass to the caterpillars
has made for an unusual silk. Tell them all
that I am sorry for my birth, that the guano plant
ate all but your tinted spectacles. Tell them

I didn't intend for my birth
to be such an affront,
but that after months
of sodium baths
I no longer bled from my gums... That I have
planted my dragon's teeth in the buttocks of Tiresias
and it was fun.

My love...

Desultory Photo with Ocean Prospect

for Chris Merrill

It is frankly something of a bait and switch
with broomstraw for daffodils, a dead sock
for a finch and all the endless auditions
of an eventual self.

One regrettable change in the program notes
will stress the poet's affection for a darkening
photograph with the slender Rimbaud
on a beach in Abyssinia, salinating
in sepia ghost, located below a grim black palm,
the tree clearly chosen
to further accent the girlish figure
of this soon-to-be-dead deliberate adolescent genius.

In the photo
he is surely somehow older, the pixels are devouring
his leg and its shadow is flexing in pain
there on the cool quartz sand of Abyssinia
or somewhere at the edge of Africa?

Please don't think you reached for me
and found the rank ulcerated leg
of a major French poet. Within the relays
of this poem it is just the opposite sleight of palm
that matters, that gives
it all away.

Please pardon the copulating snails
in the highest fronds.
I believe the French actually eat
these slugs raw with a dry tart mustard.

There is meaning in the inventories of sand.

For example, everything is feeding
everywhere, at all times.
And now for the switch —

where emptiness becomes my rhyme
for *times*. Twitching,
I said, on the cool quartz sands of far-off Abyssinia,
my motherland.

Of Art & Memory

It's odd how snow fails at totality:

falls of urine down the rose feldspar rocks.
First fog edging from the cedars
to meet the icy shoulders of the highway.

The heater is broken. The car's cold.
My father with Sinatra on the radio
is nodding off.
I move the dial for a late, vicious Scarlatti.
In truth, I too am sleepy.

My grandmother is dead.
The undertaker who is preparing her
for the viewing
thinks she is actually her younger sister
whom he adored in grammar school —   sixty-three
years ago.

After the long and unforgiving illness
Grandmother is a clean slate. Old Collins,
the mortician, who everyone
acknowledges was a genius,
will put our living great-
aunt's face there...
When *she* suffers the recognition
later that week, she'll feel flattered
just before fainting.

My brother will
catch her from behind —

and it's as if he's stringing a hammock
in a sudden wind.
If she had died in her faint,
striking her head on that pew seat
my brother collapsed into...   what
would the mortician have done then
with his best work behind him in a sister's grave?

The big mule deer in a white mantle
stepping from the fog into my father's car lights
wears some of the true
adornments of my grandmother, in particular the eyes
and a gold smoke or light
scrawled in large ellipses at her mouth and nostrils.

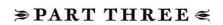

PART THREE

The Last Sentence of the Evening

> The goat gave him a funny look,
> and then pronounced an alphabet.
>
> Be the thorn, be adorned with roses.
> MEVLANA JELALUDDIN RUMI

December 21, 2001

I.

It was like, yes, your fear of oceans;
not the flood,

but the dark alphabet of its rising moon.
There in the small garden that's wet
with midnight:
a dead donkey in the desert well,
they'll say it appeared as the noon sun
done feasting on shadows...   *no,*

the poor creature's teeth, at midnight,
without hands for a lamp,
were just an accident of stars
reflected in well water —
that's what these young lovers in blue cloaks
told the old grandfather, Sacchid Plover.

The sad grandfather, in exile from his country,
down from the snow of the mountain
with his important flocks. The grandfather
who once perfected with his favorite goat
an alphabet of its own invention. It was
somewhat nasal
with a rubbery septum.

Over time the goat talked too much—
was sacrificed to God.

   2.

Well, if not to God, then to a first banquet
of the winter
with sweet fists of wild rice and a pink cauliflower.
The grandfather repeating, "The death
of another language must always
be celebrated."

So, Mevlana, you are amazed at what
a hillside friend confided to you,
that his captive cheetah is quite content
to eat cheese and nothing else.

It's unacceptable since your very own son,
jealous
and with the encouragement of the whole town,
called your dearest friend to the back door,
cutting his throat right there
with a sharpened arbor knife,
then dragging the corpse
to a cemetery well
with its long black mica curbstone.

It was a deep and voluntary well.

Your slain friend, Shams,
his spirit that is,
indulged the shy lovers, their breasts nearly bare
under the fat stars,
but he failed to bemuse those children at noon

who knew, at a distance,
the smell of a dead donkey down a well.

I think the sins of our children
are passed to the fathers? It explains
so much. Kira, your wife,
thinks this isn't right—   does a saint
sit with the dogs at the door of blood?

Your neighbor's abused camels are coughing
in their meal of chaff. The old female
kneels with sores at her knees and mouth.

The eccentric holy man, Shams, now
returned to you from Damascus,
vanishes at your back door.
The other neighbor's hairless pup
begins to bark. And you feel a stabbing
at your heart. *You said nothing.*

You finished a hemistich of dream,
two maybe,
and almost heard a new spoony melody.

You began scribbling a thousand verses
for the yellow dates
ripening in a high palm under the graveyard moon.

You wrote that each tear
reaching your beard reflected that moon
just beyond an arched window that was greenish...

Later, when the murdering son died
you refused to attend his burial. *Poor Indogen,
your Shams has vanished.*

Damascus, it is written, will vanish
like so many boiling tangerines
bursting the amethyst skyline.

   3.
How long, they asked, is the tail
of the dog who sleeps with our lepers?

Not so brief that it stares
at what isn't there.

Not so long
that it runs on to envy,

or nostalgia.

   4.
Sad Shams's bamboo flute was glorified
and missed after he vanished...
then the wind, through an eye socket
of his skull, sighed.

Ah, surprise...

The infidels had turned the very earth
of the far cemetery
while looking for jewelry and gold teeth
that could not total, as treasure,
his father's one marbleized eye of opal
plucked from the mummified cadaver.

Lauds, white Ibis and the harbor
of burning ships...
She passed the night forming triangles
of unequal sides. There was a day-meeting of women
at the millrace. They agreed
to feed us, again:

Mother Azra'il as the spring messenger
with her mustard jar and black writing quill.
Women in faded red shrouds spinning
in the ruined lodges...

A bad vision after feasting?
The wind moves farther along
touching the tall reeds of a pond: small locust
sailing over the water:

                Mustafa, excellent perikleitos, Jesus
and more burning pallets of straw.

Please never repeat for anyone
what I am about to tell you all:

     5.
With the sudden death of a young dervish,
the father came and asked Rumi,
"How should I bury my son —   in the earth,
or with a box-elder casket?" The oldest
disciple answered,
"How was he suckled? At your breast,

or at his mother's?"

6.

The seven sleepers
have cleared the radiant field of stones.
Sacchid Plover talks to the new lamb. Its white coat
perfumed with ozone.

This is the shortest day. On the full moon
I'll make an offering
of pomegranates to my windowsill.

The lamb screams. Jupiter grows fatter.

Sacchid Plover sails out in a basket
over the sea. Is he
the third sleeper whom we were
never introduced to that peaceful evening?

The beggar said to him,
a war is always a paradox of cliques, each
missing a stitch to the other. Then,
she spat. He responded while standing
deep in spring snow:

It's about suffering, Mistress,
it talks us up in the morning
and smooths the forehead at night.

It's a caution of Egyptian bread and soup
at bedtime.
If it's absent, I trust nothing.

La was right —   it's a cold unexpected
splash or trill of breast milk
to the cheek and forehead, a gloriole

of clear stone and fat, slapping against
the eye that is turning blue with it.

La also said, "With luck, the two
red kittens
licking your face are the happiness
that suffering must instruct…"
dead-bang mallet, sack of rocks.

The master has harvested calamus flowers from snow.

He has sucked blood from an egg
while the other hand-danced with trout.
He's the one-legged prayer
of the laklak —   the blue stork
who is leaving us at winter solstice, et cetera…

He might be
the reader of the last sentence —   we look to him
for something —   the screen door
of a farmhouse banging shut
near the back by the frozen compost —

gradually, all the lights are put out.

7.

summer 1949

My great-grandmother in a plaited paper gown
crosses a field in the Vermont mountains.
Her cow, La,

follows behind her manufacturing
spectacular packets of dark manure.

I smell a sweet gladiola pool.
She and her cow are frightening the silver-blue

locust as they come.
I am in the grass by the iron pump, just

four years old, and dumb
by calculation —   no reader
of sentences.

Here is where
my great-grandfather built a large pond
as provision against fire in our outer barns.

He ran a gated canal from the river
through two fields of goldenrod
to the long hollow of alfalfa.
When he was finished, he said, *Bright Pond!*

That slim silhouette of heron
standing out in the middle of it
is dumber than I was. But
he's the boss now. And he is done
reciting verse for us
here in the charged air of the evening:

his hooded eyes are slowly, slowly
closing but nothing
has really changed that clearly,
except for the sun having set
behind the mountain,
leaving us in a half-light that is sacred
to our dear friend, poet and mystic, Jelaluddin

Rumi.

Late in the Three Periods of No Thought

First, an obese sunbeam of the minor white.

A word never before spoken
by the poet. The broken tenement windows
like leaves gone silly
in the spilled light between
two platinum wet trees.
A measure of reciprocity

in old bread and meat.
One of the great Lin-chi monks
bringing back to China
the noodle sutra; hardships

like hundred-watt bulbs
in the ankles and elbows.

Arthritic and radiant
in a brooding spring deluge,
a younger version of Vasubandhu
is moving his bowels
between two tulip trees —

just for a moment,
he sees a ruin of yellow buildings,
in Poughkeepsie; he thinks
last night was the moon
of swallowing a torn rag
soaked in linseed. No, it was

a feast moon of dried wheat and worms.
Small white worms
now shitting in Vasubandhu's mouth.

Vasubandhu in a sodden sunbeam.
All morning the little permissions

                    being written out...

The Mandala Keeper

The broken chalk of lightning
across the thrashing trees
makes a saliva of the rain
flung to the streets.
All he can think of in a suddenly blackened room
is the ethyl spirits
of radishes cracking between his teeth,
the louver of tongue finding in its acid
a silver foil that's falling
past the gullet to his stomach.

The downed power lines snake
through the sump bubble of a suburban lawn
with the bloodied pedigree of hairline
on some Naga queen who loathes
the hearts of children
even in her easy sleep
near the bottom of a poisoned pond.

The rain calls, seems to have made a mistake
at the window.
A truck is approaching through the hill mud...

His daughters are gone to a neighboring state,
the yellow dog is dead of diabetes,
his wife in a wild burl of linen
is not awake with the storm
but with a new husband
who snores with almost
cardiac intermissions which she counts...

The keeper of the simple fears of people
in his room also counts
the many eighth-miles of silence
between lightning and its thunder —
he knows the distant autumn storm has turned
out by the cold harbor, is passing
back through itself
like young sleepers who begin to touch:

her long hair in his mouth, her rose thumb
crossing his white stomach;
they wake to a dream they believed
they were falling from...

the keeper, who invented their slumber,
wishes for them
the long fragrance of summer days,
more love,
and all the splendid expected human plunder
of this age, no different than any other.

Dementia

I had located the reflecting pines in the dark glass
of my husband's backyard.
It was then that this hen the size of a house said,
"Ruth, it's a bargain. Listen, girlfriend,
take the cruise: Alaskan crab, foie gras, and bare-assed rabbit
in some purple sauce."

Our students were brilliant that winter.

I said, somewhat in the direction of the hen,
"Go to hell. You are just a giant fowl
harassing us." In the red breast of the thing
was my dead husband patiently polishing our silverware.

The beautiful thing about a cruise, I added
with sarcasm, is that everything gets nailed down —
even the handsome men
with vodka tonics, gypsy vermouth and gin...

hen hen hen   *loose lose crews*

en en en   *use use use*

enruse enruse enruse!

In the diabolic *Webster's Fifth,* ENRUSE:

of Anglo-Saxon derivation; the complex preparations
of a very certain deception.
A new word for my husband.

(Even a long nail through the dentures on the bedside table.
Even sleep with a stake through its meat.)

While in college, my breasts
were nearly polished with their frustrations.

The thing about the backyard
is that it's begun snowing again. The tablecloth
is immaculate. They have stapled the bib to my sternum
and I am tear-assing through Alaskan crabs like a red hen

the size of my house. *Shh, shh.*

We woke the wood mouse again. He's the one
with the book that is full of words
and meanings for words.
Which suggests every book
is a dictionary, every bikini a moose.

It won't stop snowing.
Henshit drifting into the kitchen. The husband patiently
collecting it
for his sweet little garden with its bold border of glads,
that delphinium, and mustard.

I think it's time you apologized
to me. The giant king crabs, heated pink and spotted,
are eating us alive.

Is this just what you had in mind, mister?

                                            Alive. Alive.

Ars Poetica: A Stone Soup

There's the obese three-quarters moon of Aquinas
obsessed with the burning crescent
that will, within days, complete it! There's
the very confidence of stone soup
offered, in a gentlemanly contract,
to the dead farmer's wife.

And, here, the mean ratio of all other
ingredients (leeks, venison, potato, beans,
net of spices, and whole cream)
must not outweigh the beggar's alchemical
contribution of the worn limestone weight,

                                        yes, that simple stone
bearing, at the least, something
of the salts of a long-dead sea.

There are those who, in my poor homily, will
leave the table pleased
with the wisdom and generosity of the widow:

her shared meal, his clump
of wildflowers, the springwater he brought
from the next county, and a heavy salt almost of history;
others, of course, leave the table feeling cheated —
mistaking the sum of the parts, even
the absence of carrots,
for a mysteriously minor whole.

To rescue these sad calculators from themselves
and from any suggestion

of a secret vulgarity in my poem
(as if it were my burden to welcome them
to the simple loss of all excuse),

I'll quote my friend, the poet Marvin Bell,
"Every poem is an ars poetica."

What else?

Elegy for a Fallen Brother, Composed in the First Month of Winter

Dried dark leaves of moxa
mixed with gunpowder. The monk
lights a braid of six centimeters
dusted with phosphorus.

Getting up with the sickness
he thought to try this cure,
which, he confides to his disciple,
killed the beloved Master Kukei.

Master Kukei, who, though dead,
grinned for twelve days and nights
without corruption or a simple stench —
Just sitting there beside the white table
with stones on it.

A wandering monk of no sense
said that in this dark time
he recognized the Master's grin
as effortless, as
belonging to a child of privilege
who has dropped a hot yellow turd
onto a spidery plate of cold bone
while, in the poor light, crackpot Taoists
gather through the night to study it.

Perhaps, this is why our monk fully doubled
the measure of gunpowder for his medicine —
startling a cloud of blackbirds
up out of a dozen bare peach orchards.

The birds lifting like the Duke's tattered banners
over an insane horse that had pulled cannon
out over the frozen river
to where three villages are still burning,
rain and snow visible at a distance
but still beyond the barrier of sand and sticks
that made no difference.

Afterword to a Quartet:
Vision of a Tibetan Master Walking over Snow

With the angle of light
it might not be snow, rather
an immense salt field
with dark chromium lakes
under a day moon.

The zombie
borrowed from the local charnel ground
is made nervous
by the violet and rust tinctures
of vulture excrement falling all about him;
he runs out ahead of the Master
carrying heavy blocks of scripture,
a bolt of green silk,
and the large sack of salt with the Master's
teacher's bald head preserved in it.

There is no barley or brick of tea — neither
of these men need eat or drink.

The earth is moving with them,
sudden sinkholes, pomegranate red,
escalate the landscape. This quake
is unforgiving. In Lhasa,
a girl stabs her forearm
with a gold and turquoise hairpin
to keep from fainting
while she ushers her charges, six
aristocratic schoolboys,
out of the ginger house into the gardens.

Master Gedün Chopël
has a leathery yellow leech
on his forehead, is
examining the scene before him
laughing at how the earth is now cratered,
a reflection of the day moon
that is stalking them.

The zombie complains to his dead mother
about a telegraph of pain in his arthritic elbow.
This is the arm that says the beads, rounded
bone clicking twice in the wrist
then tumbling to his shoulder.

It is the ache of winter,
the occult polyphoenix warmth of deserts
rising with it. Not unlike
the Master's secret pleasure pavilion —
its walls, blue and red
with spirals, whole declensions of universes
multiplying like the rings
of colored heat that leave the bodies of two
blackened lovers who are
the pivot, weight, and perspective
of the room.

Their canines are exaggerated
like the low ladling of her knobby spine.

Here there is no naked bearded man
seated high in a tree
being tortured by barbarians
who have architected stone
and water into an eternal city.
There is

a spear thrust into the side of the young teacher,
to remind us of the marriage of the flesh.

Lama Chopël laughs again,
again causing the earth to move;
he thinks, the Jesus
was a great being, great bodhiset,

raised from the dead, but not like the zombie
floating out ahead of the Teacher,
a virtual cosmic beast of burden, blue tapers
of ice hanging with his beard,
the Jesus Lord
carrying a planet and its genius for bacteria
in a stained sack of salt down the musical ellipse
of a minor solar system inching
across a minor district of suns now governed
by alien dolphin kings and
a darker lizard prince who think they know
just how and when
it all will end, how
and when it was all somehow beginning...

The Fish Cipher of Michel de Nostradam

The virgin's breast with milk leaving it
lit by a fire of sticks
is what the King admits
to seeing seconds before
his horse's steps minced
the bone-yellow lint of the spring air.

It lifts his helmet's visor to limits,
a golden spear
halving the eye's landscape —

a valley of cypress
flagging the night
beyond the green toxic jelly
of the dyer's ponds.

Peasants dressed in woolen sock
struggling past the aqueduct
shoulder a painting
of hilltop monasteries burning
in snow.

The air so cold that it snaps
like the leg of a horse weighted with sacks
of souring meats and gold.

The falling moon shrieks at us.
An elder dyer's son
nailed to a tree by the landlord.

A ship out on the green sea
bobs under its flag of plague.

All of the meek neighborhoods emptying,
the children
memorizing with their voices
the coarse alarms. A comet

crossed above the old caves, below
the nests and skulls that crown
the pasturage.

The one god of the kingdom
dressed in a blacksmith's apron
eats even
his beard and cheese with cruelty.
He sweats both salt and snowflakes.

The aching ropes of the ship
mock the young woman
in the shepherd's hut
who is giving birth to twins, one alive—

one not. The Muslim butcher coughs twice,
spraying a blood of dubious origin
across the open eyes
of a sunken sow's head—

the wife, never superstitious, thinks
that even in future worlds, this husband
must be recognized for an absorbed master

of the business of business. Abundant
fear now
lifted like mirrors everywhere in the town,
and we must see the darker prophecies
as a simple choosing
of something over something else.

Revelation of a Winter's Night

for Peter Junker

1.

It's one of those moments when you look
from what you thought was a book
to speak to someone
who has quietly left the dark room.

2.

Breathing, sudden latches of cold air —
who is there?

3.

The mouse with the yellow berry of cereal
in its mouth stops on a stair.

4.

It was first light touching the snow —
that's what startled you.

Ancestral

for Cynthia Hunter

The wet polish of horizon
rising like a waterline
in the porcelain tub. For the moment
first light makes white sponge
of the trees, rocks, and trafficking grouse.

The stream suddenly runs without its voices.

Your bare back in glossy cuneiform,
a clay talc of breast making arcs
above the red blanket that an exposed leg
weights against wind.

I ask your name without waking.

I hear the stream again,
pods rattling in the trees above us —

the tub spills over
into the empty room
of an empty house never before seen

by either of us.

Riddle

The snow lifts into the beards of sycamores.
Laura says with some nervousness
that the tracks over the snow
are divisible only by their sum and zero.

An owl, leaving its cedar bough, laughs. I laugh.

She breaks a stick, says that a brazen mathematics
of stars in the illustrated night
is signaling its approval to us.

I say, "Oh, really? And which stars are these,
precisely?"

Childlike, with a sigh, she points and whispers,
"That little blue one, in Orion,
just beyond the stomach
of the hunter and his trapezium.
What do you think, how many wars
in our new millennium will reach
their natural conclusions, and blink?"

About the Author

Norman Dubie was born in Barre, Vermont, in April 1945. His poems have appeared in many magazines, including *American Poetry Review, Antaeus, The Paris Review, The New Yorker, Poetry, TriQuarterly,* and *Field.* He has won the Bess Hokin Award of the Modern Poetry Association and fellowships from the Ingram Merrill Foundation, the John Simon Guggenheim Memorial Foundation, and the National Endowment for the Arts. Mr. Dubie won the PEN USA prize for best poetry collection in 2001. He has recently published a book-length futurist work, *The Spirit Tablets at Goa Lake,* with *Blackbird,* the online magazine of *The New Virginia Review.* He lives in Tempe, Arizona, with the cat Fast–Eddy–Smoky–Chokyi Lodrö, and teaches at Arizona State University.

The Chinese character for poetry is made up of two parts: "word" and "temple." It also serves as pressmark for Copper Canyon Press.

Founded in 1972, Copper Canyon Press remains dedicated to publishing poetry exclusively, from Nobel laureates to new and emerging authors. The Press thrives with the generous patronage of readers, writers, booksellers, librarians, teachers, students, and funders—everyone who shares the conviction that poetry invigorates the language and sharpens our appreciation of the world.

MAJOR FUNDING HAS BEEN PROVIDED
BY THE FOLLOWING ORGANIZATIONS:

The Allen Foundation for The Arts

Lannan Foundation

National Endowment for the Arts

The Starbucks Foundation

Washington State Arts Commission

For information and catalogs:

COPPER CANYON PRESS
Post Office Box 271
Port Townsend, Washington 98368
360/385-4925
www.coppercanyonpress.org

THE ALLEN FOUNDATION *for* THE ARTS

The text of this book is set in ITC Bodoni Six™ Book, a font designed by
Sumner Stone, Jim Parkinson, Holly Goldsmith, and Janice Fishman in
1994, after research on the original steel punches of Giambattista Bodoni
(1740–1813). The titles are set in MVB Sirenne® by Alan Dague-Greene and
Mark van Bronkhorst. Sirenne was inspired by engraved captions from a 1719
natural history, Louis Renard's *Poissons, ecrevisses et crabes,* which includes
an engraving of a mermaid (*sirenne*) captured and kept alive for four days
in a tub of water. Book design and composition by Valerie Brewster, Scribe
Typography. Printed on archival-quality Glatfelter Author's Text at
McNaughton & Gunn.